NATIONAL GEOGRAPHIC

Stories From the
UNDERGROUND RAILROAD

PIONEER EDITION

By Peter Winkler

CONTENTS

Eyewitness on the UNDERGROUND RAILROAD

History owes a lot to William Still.
He helped hundreds of runaway slaves.
And he recorded their amazing stories.

BY PETER WINKLER

William Still

Can one person change the lives of many? William Still did. He helped hundreds of people find freedom.

Still worked on the **Underground Railroad.** This "railroad" did not have trains. It was a group of people. They helped slaves escape.

Still helped about 800 slaves. He gave them money, food, and clothing. He found them places to stay. Still did something else too. He listened.

People told Still about their lives. He kept careful notes. He created an **oral history.** That is a record of people's stories. His notes grew into a book. It was called *The Underground Rail Road.* The stories that follow are from Still's book. They are stories of freedom.

WILLIAM AND ELLEN CRAFT

Slaves rarely escaped from states in the far South. They had too far to travel. Most **fugitives** were caught. But William and Ellen Craft found a way to escape.

Ellen's skin was pale, almost white. So she dressed up like a white man. She rode the train north. William rode along. He acted like Ellen's slave.

The plan worked! No one guessed their secret. They reached Philadelphia safely. Then off came Ellen's glasses and hat. People were amazed by the trick!

After a rest, the Crafts moved to Boston. They spent two years there. Then their old master hired slave hunters to find them. So they moved to England. They lived there happily for the next 20 years.

Badge worn by freed slaves in Charleston, South Carolina

Wordwise

fugitive: runaway

oral history: eyewitness stories and memories told to an interviewer

Underground Railroad: informal web of people who helped slaves escape

Henry "Box" Brown

Henry Brown was a slave. He lived in Virginia. He knew most slaves ran away on foot. He also knew hunters often caught them. So Brown tried something different.

Brown got a wooden box. It was three feet long and two feet wide. It stood two and a half feet high.

Brown lined the box with cloth. He wanted it to be just right. He was planning on squeezing into the box!

Brown drilled holes for air. He put water and food into the box. Next he climbed inside. A friend shipped it to Pennsylvania. The train trip took 26 hours.

William Still and others opened the box. Then Brown popped out. No one could believe their eyes.

Brown spent a few days with Underground Railroad workers. Then he moved to Boston. There he worked to end slavery.

THE GRANGER COLLECTION, NEW YORK (ESCAPE); COURTESY OF THE LEVI COFFIN HOUSE AND WAYNET (DOLL); MARK THIESSEN (DOCUMENT, MEMO PAD, AND PENCIL)

October 1857

"THE MEMORABLE TWENTY-EIGHT"

Aaron Cornish was a slave. His master promised to set him free. But he never wrote the promise down. When the master died, Cornish remained a slave.

Cornish and his wife decided to escape. So did many of their friends. All in all, there were 17 adults and 11 children. They left Maryland during a storm.

Rain made it hard for hunters to follow them. But traveling through the storm was not easy. Children got sick. Everyone got hungry. But they all kept walking.

The journey was hard. Yet no one gave up. Not even the children wanted to turn back.

Step by step, the group marched to Philadelphia. They were sick and hungry. They had no money. But they made it!

In Philadelphia, people gave the runaways clothes and food. The 28 slaves also got their freedom.

Rag doll from the Civil War era

Ask. Listen. Write.

William Still created an oral history of the Underground Railroad. An oral history is a collection of memories. They are told aloud. Most slaves could not read or write. So they told their stories to Still. Then he wrote them down.

You can create an oral history of your community. Start by talking to a relative or neighbor near you. To begin, make a list of questions.

UNDERGROUND RAIL ROAD

A RECORD
OF
FACTS, AUTHENTIC NARRATIVES, LETTERS, &c.,
Narrating the Hardships Hair-breadth Escapes and Death Struggles
OF THE
Slaves in their efforts for Freedom,
AS RELATED
BY THEMSELVES AND OTHERS, OR WITNESSED BY THE AUTHOR;
TOGETHER WITH
SKETCHES OF SOME OF THE LARGEST STOCKHOLDERS, AND
MOST LIBERAL AIDERS AND ADVISERS,
OF THE ROAD.

BY
WILLIAM STILL,
For many years connected with the Anti-Slavery Office in Philadelphia, and Chairman
of the Acting Vigilant Committee of the Philadelphia Branch of
the Underground Rail Road.

Illustrated with 70 fine Engravings by Bensell, Schell and others, and
Portraits from Photographs from Life.

Thou shalt not deliver unto his master the servant that has escaped from his master unto thee.—Deut. xxiii. 15.

ONLY BY SUBSCRIPTION.

ADELPHIA;
& COATES,
UT STREET.

Oral History Tips

- **Ask questions where the answer is more than just "yes" or "no."**

- **Start some questions with the five W's: Who? What? Where? When? Why?**

- **Ask for details. For instance, what sounds or smells does the person remember about the past?**

- **Ask the person to give examples of how things have changed.**

- **Toward the end of the interview, ask if there was anything you should have asked but did not. This can lead to interesting stories.**

Interview Questions

Journey

100 DOLLARS REWARD!

Runaway from the subscriber on the 27th of July, my Black Woman, named **EMILY,** Seventeen years of age, well grown, black color, has a whining voice. She took with her one dark calico and one blue and white dress, a red corded gingham bonnet; a white striped shawl and slippers. I will pay the above reward if taken near the Ohio river on the Kentucky side, or **THREE HUNDRED DOLLARS,** if taken in the State of Ohio, and delivered to me near Lewisburg, Mason County, Ky. **THO'S. H. WILLIAMS.** August 4, 1853.

This notice offers a reward for a runaway slave.

Slavery was legal in southern states. It was not allowed in northern states, Canada, or Mexico. So runaway slaves often traveled hundreds of miles to reach freedom.

Slaves took many routes to find freedom. Some slaves traveled south. They marched through Texas to Mexico. They escaped by boat from Florida.

Many others traveled north. They followed the Underground Railroad. Some fled to northern states. Some made it to Canada. Others traveled all the way to England.

Hunted North and South

Their journeys were long and risky. Runaways were often caught and sent back. That is because of a law. It was called the Fugitive Slave Act.

The law said that slaves must be returned to their owners. Even if they made it to a "free" state!

Slave states and free states argued over the law. The fight over slavery led to the Civil War. When the war ended, all slaves were freed. Today, their stories remind us of how important freedom is.

This group of runaway slaves worked together to find freedom.

to Freedom

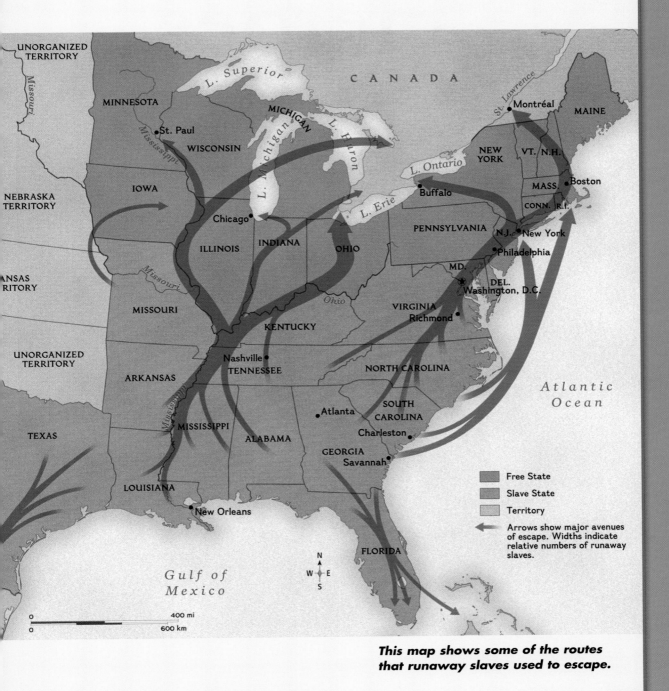

UNORGANIZED
TERRITORY

Missouri

L. Superior

C A N A D A

St. Lawrence

MINNESOTA

MICHIGAN

L. Huron

Montréal

MAINE

St. Paul

WISCONSIN

L. Michigan

NEW
YORK

VT. N.H.

Mississippi

NEBRASKA
TERRITORY

IOWA

L. Ontario

MASS.

Boston

Buffalo

CONN.

R.I.

Chicago

PENNSYLVANIA

N.J.

New York

ANSAS
RITORY

ILLINOIS

INDIANA

OHIO

L. Erie

Philadelphia

Missouri

MD.

Ohio

DEL.
Washington, D.C.

MISSOURI

KENTUCKY

VIRGINIA
Richmond

UNORGANIZED
TERRITORY

Nashville

NORTH CAROLINA

ARKANSAS

TENNESSEE

Atlanta

SOUTH
CAROLINA

Atlantic
Ocean

TEXAS

MISSISSIPPI

Mississippi

ALABAMA

Charleston

GEORGIA
Savannah

LOUISIANA

New Orleans

Free State

Slave State

Territory

Arrows show major avenues
of escape. Widths indicate
relative numbers of runaway
slaves.

FLORIDA

N
W E
S

Gulf of
Mexico

0   400 mi
0   600 km

*This map shows some of the routes
that runaway slaves used to escape.*

Underground Heroes

OHIO HISTORICAL SOCIETY (BOTH)

Rhoda Jones was a member of the Underground Railroad in Ohio.

Runaway slaves faced lots of dangers. So did the people who helped them. Many people took great risks to help slaves. Who were these heroes of the Underground Railroad?

Working Against Slavery

They were people from every walk of life. Some were freed or escaped slaves. Some worked for churches. Some were from the North. Others were from the South. Each had different reasons for helping. Yet they all thought slavery was wrong.

Risks of the Railroad

Helping runaways was dangerous. People could be fined or put in jail. Some even lost their lives.

Yet many people like Rhoda Jones took the risk. She lived in Ohio. Some people there had been killed for helping slaves. Still, she opened her home to slaves.

Jones was one of the thousands who helped. Members of the Underground Railroad did not get paid. Most never became famous. Yet they did what they could. They helped people find freedom.

These twenty men were arrested for helping just one slave escape.

UNDERGROUND RAILROAD

Answer these questions to find out what you learned from the book.

1 What was the Underground Railroad?

2 Who was William Still? How did he help people find freedom?

3 How did some people escape from slavery?

4 Why was escaping from slavery dangerous?

5 How can oral history help people learn about the past?

STEPHEN R. WAGNER